First published in 2020

© Lex Johnson

Design by Liam Johnson

ISBN: 978-0-6488832-0-3

1. Australia – History
2. Tasmania – History

Title: No Map to Show the Way

Author: Lex Johnson, 1932 –

Editor: Linda Seaborn (nee Johnson), 1965 –

Publisher: Linda Seaborn

Cover Art: Photography by Shirley Johnson
and Design by Liam Johnson

NO MAP
— to —
SHOW THE WAY

LEX JOHNSON

Dedicated to the memory of Margaret Long (1943–2017), without whose persistence and fascination with local history, this story would never have come together.

PREFACE

Terre de Diemen (1807) Engraving by C.A. Lesueur

The core of my subject is the exploration, mapping and naming of Frederick Hendrik Bay by Abel Tasman in 1642; but a recognition of the context in which the events took place contributes to an understanding of them.

I have difficulty with the word 'discover' in relation to this exploration. In the introduction to his book Great Southern Land (2005), Professor Michael Pearson writes:

> "…in this study, if the term 'discovery' is used at all, it is in the context of the discovery of geographical or scientific facts for European science and commerce, not in the sense of the discovery of previously unknown land…"

I intend to maintain the same practice. It seems odd to talk of 'discovering' a land that has been occupied by other people for tens of thousands of years.

I suppose after that long a time, they feel it is as if they had always been here – which is the belief of Tasmanian Aborigines.

The simplest response I have heard to the idea of land 'discovery', was in a 1980s Tasmanian Film Unit documentary about Cape Barren Island, when Aboriginal elder and local character Jim Everett says:

> "We weren't 'discovered' because we weren't lost. We just didn't know you white fellas were looking for us."

– Lex Johnson (No Map to Show the Way U3A talk– circa 2006)

I acknowledge the Tasmanian Aboriginal people, as the owners of this land lutruwita. I pay my respects to the hundreds of generations of ancestors who walked and lived on these beautiful lands, to their elders and activists, past, present and emerging. This land was never ceded.

– Linda Seaborn

CONTENTS

LEX AND MARGARET
UNCOVER THE STORY

When Lex and Shirley Johnson moved to Boomer Bay in 1993, they reunited with old family friend Margaret Long.

Margaret, an ex-teacher, had taken up researching local history. The area around Boomer Bay was significant because many of the early Dutch, English and French explorers had passed through.

Lex joined her in this research.

Each year the local history group would meet at the Tasman monument in Imlay St, Dunalley. The monument was located near town to make it accessible, and in the general location of the likely first landing of Europeans from the Tasman expedition. The group would read excerpts from the Tasman expedition ship's log.

On 2 December 1642 two ship's boats with 17 people, under the commands of Senior Navigator Visscher and Supercargo Gilsemans, rowed through Marion Narrows into Blackman Bay, near present day Dunalley, and across to a creek to gather plant samples and look for fresh water.

In the 1920s through 1930s there was considerable argument in historical circles about the location of the watering site. None of the expedition maps showed it, and this is another reason that the

Local History Group at the Tasman monument, Dunalley (Photo: Shirley Johnson)
Lex Johnson, Keith Ward, Boomer (dog), Margaret Long, Susan James (sitting), Gaye Hawkes, Joan Long

THIS MONUMENT

WAS ERECTED BY THE GOVERNMENT OF TASMANIA
IN 1942 TO COMMEMORATE THE TERCENTENARY
OF THE DISCOVERY OF THIS ISLAND IN 1642
BY HON. ABEL JANS TASMAN

SHIPS BOATS COMMANDED BY
PILOT MAJOR VISSCHER
VISITED THIS BAY ON
DECEMBER 3RD 1642.

"THIS BAY" is Blackman Bay (not East Bay where the monument is situated). The date in the last line should be Dec. 2nd.

Tasman monument, Dunalley (Photo: Shirley Johnson)

monument erected in 1942, was located in the town of Dunalley, rather than the actual site.

Margaret thought it likely that the logical place to have looked for water was Boomer Creek, located bottom left in the picture below of Blackman Bay.

This creek flowed along the northern boundary of the property Lex and Shirley were living on. It was a short walk from their house to the outflow of the creek into the bay. At least once a year Margaret would turn up and coax Lex into exploring the creek, saying "this could have been it you know".

What they didn't know was that in 1932 a Dutch printer who specialised in old maps in private collections, published a map on which was marked (in Dutch) "Water Place". It was a map drawn by Isaac Gilsemans, of the Zeehaen, from the Tasman Expedition.

Aerial view of Blackman Bay (Photographer unknown)

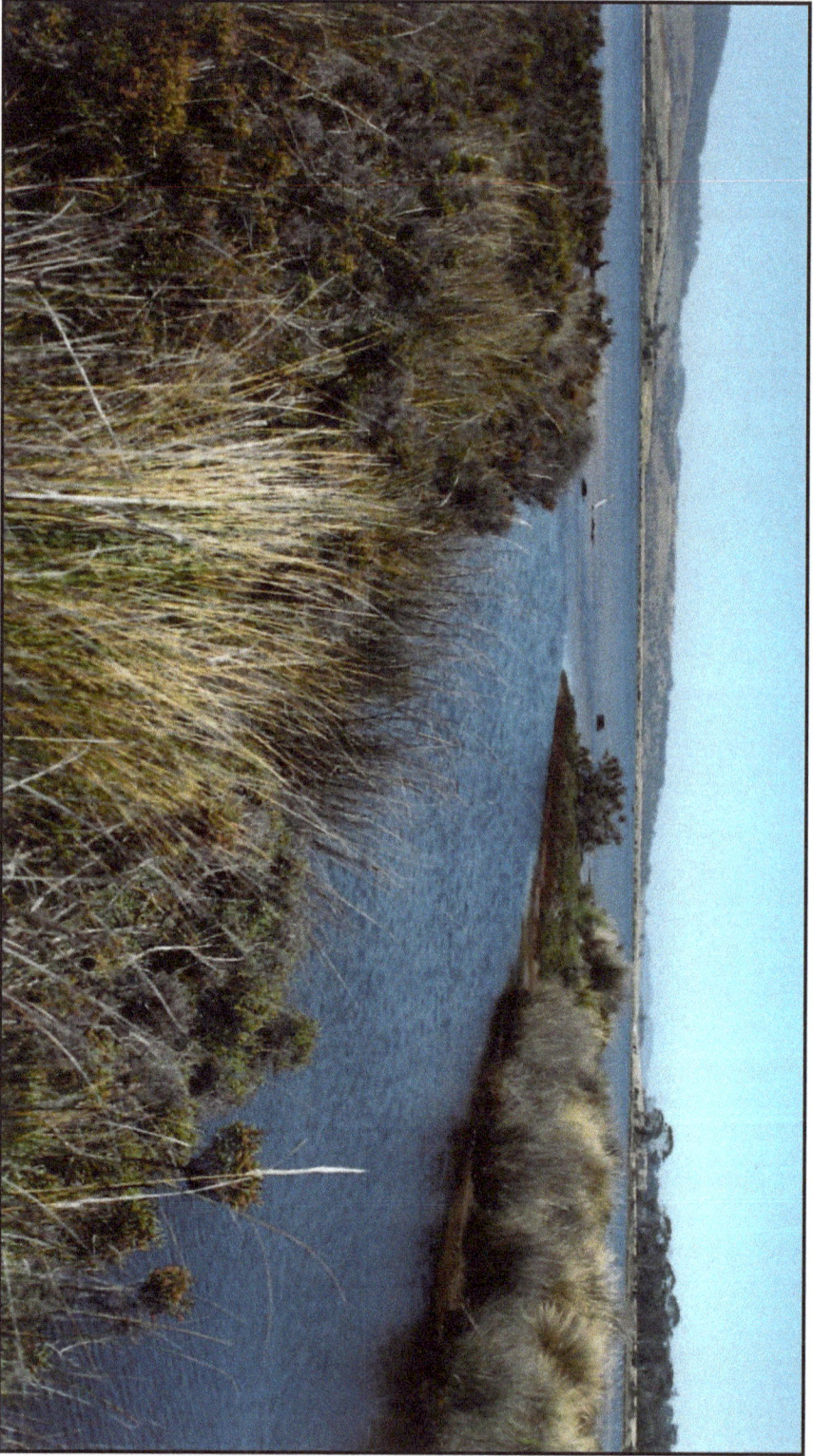

Boomer Creek outlet (Photo: Shirley Johnson)

14

Isaac Gilsemans was officially "Supercargo" (Superintendent of the cargo), or merchant in charge of trading with other countries and people encountered. As there was no call for his expertise in that field, he fell back on his ability as a mapmaker, which is probably why he was selected for the job anyway.

The map came into the possession of the Tasmanian Royal Society in December 1942 when a copy was obtained from the Royal Society in NSW. Of little importance to European or NSW people who saw it, was the small notation "Water Plaats" meaning water place, which identified the long-disputed site at which water was obtained by the exploratory party on 2 December 1642, three hundred years earlier.

That information narrowed the subject area to a small section of the western shoreline of Blackman Bay. From 1942-46 under the auspices of the Royal Society, Dr Winifred Curtis and Janet Somerville undertook a study of saltmarsh vegetation around Blackman Bay. It proved (botanically) that only the saltmarsh at the outlet of Boomer Creek supported the two types of plants identified in the Journal as being collected at the Water Place.

Concurrently A. L. Meston conducted experiments in rowing times, which showed that a return trip from the ship's anchorage to Boomer Creek, plus time for water collection and some exploration, reasonably fitted the known times of departure and return. He also put forward a plausible reason why the shape of Blackman Bay in Gilsemans' map did not match the current shape – that from a boat at sea level, the bay appears to end at Boomer Island; so the explorers did not see the two southern lobes of Blackman Bay.

It settled the long-running academic argument about the area of the first European landing in Tasmania, with the research pinpointing the precise location as Boomer Creek.

Isaac Gilsemans Original Chart of the Discovery of Tasmania , 1642

In 2006, the University of Tasmania published Somerville's work (Potts et al) and this book eventually made its way into Margaret and Lex's hands, confirming for them, the location of the "Watering Place".

There is no widely published reference material that says unequivocally, "Boomer Creek is the place where Abel Tasman's crew obtained water for the ships on 2 December 1642".

To begin to rectify this, Lex worked with the Nomenclature Board to successfully have the small bay at the outlet of Boomer Creek named Gilsemans Bay after Isaac Gilsemans, the mapmaker. The area needs a monument to recognise its historical significance – it is the first landing of Europeans in lutruwita, now known as Tasmania.

Map of Gilsemens Bay The List

ABEL TASMAN NAMES FREDERICK HENDRIK BAY

≈

The two ships of the Dutch Tasman Expedition came into view of mountains of the west coast of Tasmania on 24 November 1642. The Expedition was operating through the United East-India Company that (in the Dutch language) had the initials V.O.C.

The V.O.C. was a shareholder-funded private company formed in 1602, and by 1619 had established its Asian corporate headquarters at Batavia. It was the foremost company at the time and carried government rights and privileges including the right to exploration of unknown lands, and the claiming of unoccupied lands in the name of the Dutch head-of-state (the Statholder). This was originally Prince William of Orange, but at the time of the Tasman voyage was Prince Frederick Hendrik.

The V.O.C. was keen to find a route to the Pacific Ocean other than through the dangerous waters controlled by Spain and Portugal at The Philippines and Timor.

They were looking for raw materials to develop, or more people with whom to trade, but they also wanted to cross the Pacific to the Peru and Chile coasts in order to harass and possibly capture Spanish galleons carrying gold and silver back to Spain. In 1642 they engaged Abel Janzsoon Tasman and the ships Heemskerck and Zeehaen.

The Dutch Expedition was managed by a Ship's Council. The Commander (Tasman) was Chairman and all the officers – both ships – were permanent members. If matters of crew discipline were involved, the two Bosuns joined the Council. For navigational matters, the two Steersmen became members and the Senior Navigator (Visscher) had two votes.

There is no support for the oft-repeated claim that Abel Tasman was the first European to see the land. Commodores do not spend their time in the crow's nest near the top of the mast. A reward of a silver coin and a bottle of arack (beer) was paid to that unknown sailor.

Given the relative positions of the two ships, it was more likely to have been the store-ship ("Zeehaen") from which the two northern mountains were sighted, rather than from Tasman's "Heemskerck" which was further south. And there is no evidence that the sailor making the sighting was European. Batavia was an international crossroads port, with sailors from all over the globe, and local seamen, available for employment.

After coasting south along the west coast, they crossed the Southern Ocean from South West Cape to South East Cape. Their reference to rocks such as Pedra Branca showed that they were about 15km offshore – and that is consistent with the course plotted on one of the maps they made.

They recorded the rocky southern end of Bruny Island (The Friars) and were on the southern edge of Storm Bay when they saw what appeared to be a potentially sheltered anchorage (today's Adventure Bay). A conference involving the officers of both ships supported the idea of anchoring in the bay, but shortly after they got underway, they were hit by a sudden north-westerly storm (hence "Storm Bay") and blown out to sea to the south east.

Apart from a brief sighting of Tasman Island (which they named), and a vague idea of the mainland (which they called "South Cape" – but is now Cape Pillar), they were almost out of sight of land for the next three days, during which time they made their way north when the winds allowed.

On 1 December they sighted a promontory (now named Cape Frederick Hendrick) and beyond it found a suitable anchorage in 22 fathoms of water. That last item is important because some earlier historians claimed that the anchorage was in Blackman Bay (which has a depth of about 2 fathoms).

The V.O.C.'s Asian office at Batavia was run by the Governor van Diemen and his ten Councillors. As commander of the Expedition, which incidentally earned him the title "Honourable", Tasman's principal responsibilities were to see that the Batavia Council's instructions were carried out, and to ensure that their valuable ships and crew returned safely.

There is no doubt that, when Tasman sailed from Batavia, he had a suggestion list of names to use in the event that he found new land – and he also used the same list the next year in his charting of Northern Australia.

A few names arose from circumstance or physical description, such as Mewstone, Storm Bay and South Cape. Tasman took a small indulgence for himself in naming Tasman Island.

The Expedition confined itself to naming marine feature – islands, bays, capes, etc. Contrary to oft-repeated assertions, it did not name Mts Heemskirk and Zeehan after the ships. Anglicised versions of those names were given by Flinders in the circumnavigation in 1798.

He named the land Van Diemen's Land for the chairman of the V.O.C. Board in Batavia, and the names of other Board members for the islands on the south and east coasts. For good measure, the Governor's wife was remembered in Maria Island.

There was only one name that out-ranked all those – Frederick Hendrik, the head-of-state of the Netherlands. That name was being reserved for something grand enough – preferably where the flag-raising would take place. The site that meets those conditions is the area now occupied by North Bay, Marion Bay and Blackman Bay (the inlet) – and the flag was planted at a small cove (Tasman Bay) within North Bay.

The maps Tasman left us have the name Frederick Hendrik Bay written in such a way that (it is said) his intention is unclear; it could apply to any of the waters we now know as North Bay, Marion Bay or Blackman Bay. The other alternative is that it applies to all three.

Over the years, Tasman has been made to shoulder the blame for not clearly indicating, on his chart, exactly what waters he meant to be called Frederick Hendrik Bay. Those accusations were usually made by people who knew little about charting traditions of the time, including that no names (except those for small islands) would be written in the 'sea' area, keeping that free for plotting courses. If you intend that the name "Frederick Hendrik Bay" apply to all the waters named and you are obliged to write it only once, and write it on the land part of the map, where do you put it? The logical place is where Tasman's chart maker (Visscher) put it, on the only piece of land that touches all three parts of the one body of water.

In maritime terms, what we now call Marion Bay is not a true bay: it lacks one of the two cradling arms of significant capes or headlands. As we shall see later, subsequent explorers saw only one bay, Frederick Hendrik Bay, filling the space from Cape Bernier to Cape Frederick Hendrik.

Blackman Bay was described by early explorers as an "inlet" of the main bay. In Tasman's time, it is likely that the opening we now call Marion Narrows was much wider (as shown on his maps).

On 2 December 1642 two ship's boats with 17 people, under the commands of Senior Navigator Visscher and Supercargo Gilsemans, rowed through Marion Narrows into Blackman Bay, and across to a creek to gather plant samples and look for fresh water.

Whilst there they saw large trees with notches about five feet apart. They presumed that these notches were for climbing the trees and surmised that "the natives here must be of very tall stature".

Tasman's journal uses the pronoun "we" throughout – meaning "members of the expedition", maybe (but not necessarily) including Tasman himself. There is a single departure from that practice in the whole journal. At the ceremonial planting of the flag which Tasman could not carry out personally because rough seas prevented him landing, and the carpenter swam ashore to do it for him, the journal records:

> "Our master carpenter carried out the task he had been
> assigned as myself – Abel Tasman – Skipper Gerrit Janz,
> and Assistant Merchant Abraham Coomens looked on"
> (Discovery, Duyker, p15).

Clearly, Tasman was carrying out a legal function in claiming the land on behalf of his head-of-state, Prince Frederick Hendrik. He had personal responsibility to see that correct form was observed; and in the event of his incapacity, Skipper Gerrit Janz would become the leader of the expedition. Coomens was the official recorder who is thought to have actually written up the journal.

Thus we have the properly authorised leader, and his deputy, and the official keeper of records, legally witnessing that the land had been claimed in proper form. The place where this event took place would obviously be given the name Frederick Hendrik Bay – that is precisely why the name had been reserved until that time.

Tasman remained in the boat while the carpenter swam ashore with the flag on the afternoon of 3 December. That relatively insignificant

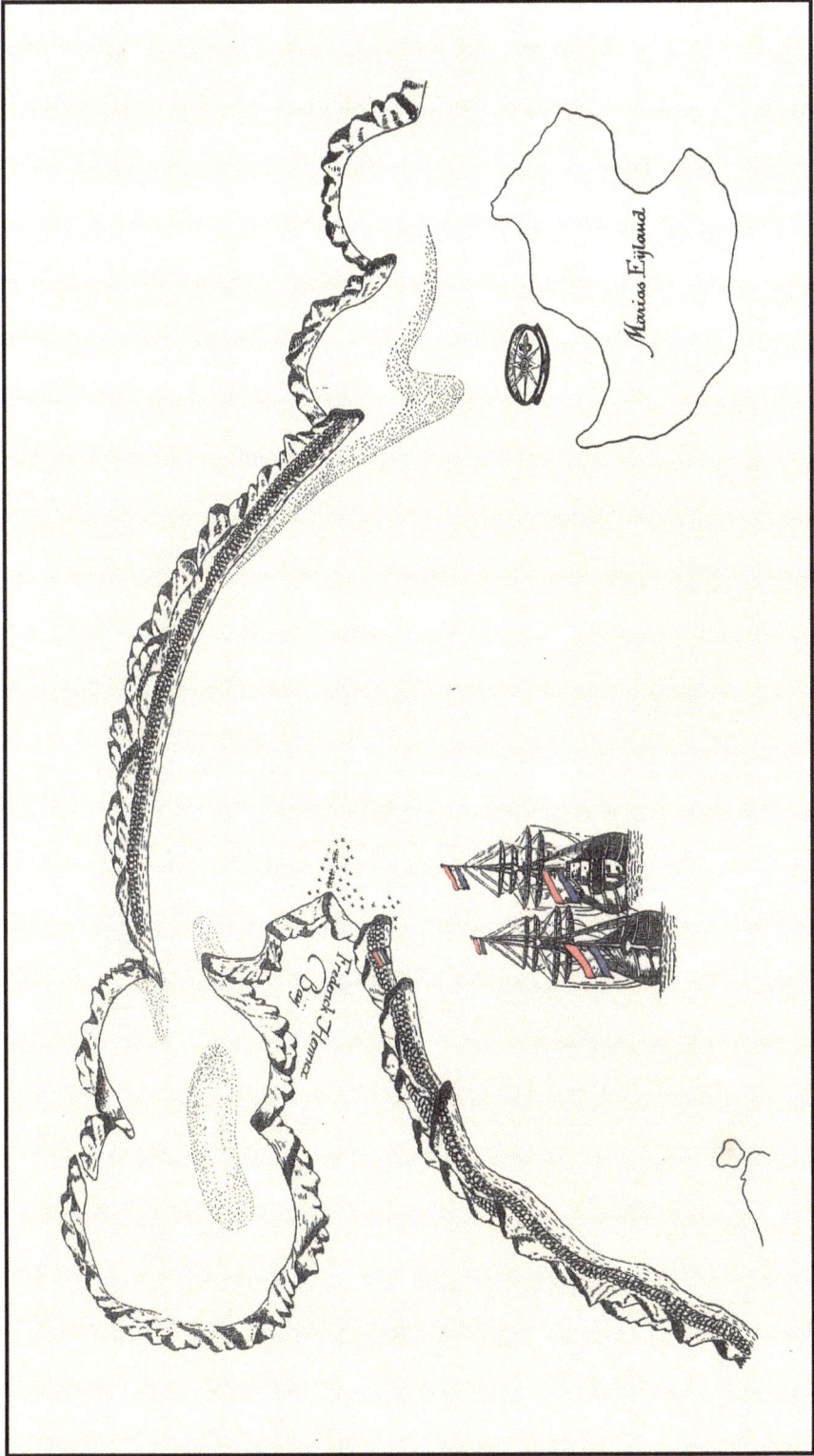

Sketch in the Journal of the Tasman Expedition, 1642

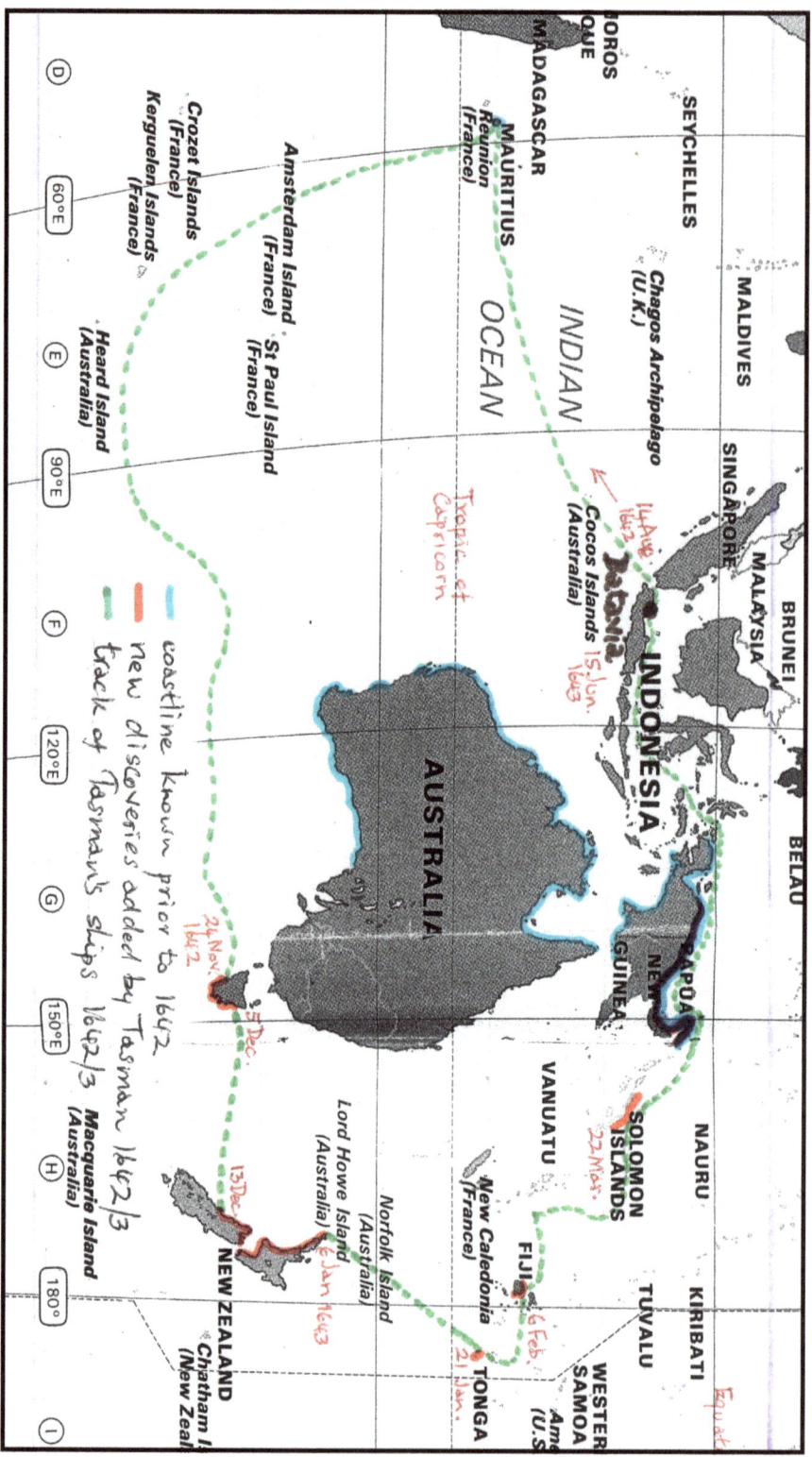

Map of the route of the Tasman Expedition, 1642 Lex Johnson

cove was not named by the Expedition – probably because it formed part of Tasman's "Frederick Hendrik Bay". Tasman saw the Bay as one magnificent sheet of water, appropriate to bear the most important name he had to bestow.

On 4 December the Heemskerk weighed anchor only to find it minus its flukes, which still lie somehwere in the bay. The Expedition then sailed north, named Maria Island, and next day turned east for New Zealand/Aotearoa (Staten Land). On 19 December they had an unfortunate incident with Maori people where four men from the Zeehaan were killed, and so did not attempt to come ashore again in New Zealand. After sailing to Tonga and Fiji and arriving back at Batavia on 14 June 1643 (10 months after leaving) they had inadvertently circumnavigated Australia.

≈ *1772* ≈

MARION DUFRESNE'S
TRAGIC VISIT

≈

When Marion Dufresne's expedition anchored, they wrote in their logbooks and diaries that they were in Tasman's anchorage in Frederick Hendrik Bay – which shows that they understood Tasman's intentions for that name.

Du Fresne left us no record of his voyage; but his companion ship's captain, Ambroise du Clesmeur, wrote an account which includes the statement:

> "The Bay of Frederick Hendrik, thus named by Tasman, measures approximately five leagues at the opening and two and a half deep."

Those measurements accord with the waters between Cape Berneir and Cape Frederick Hendrik. Du Clesmeur also left a small map showing the anchorage, and the coast between the two capes.

In this map presented in the book The Discovery of Tasmania (edited by Edward Duyker) the map shown is titled in English "Du Clesmeur's chart of Marion Bay..." whereas Du Clesmeur's writing at the top of the map clearly names it "Plan de la Baye Frederic Henri" (see further information in Appendix).

26

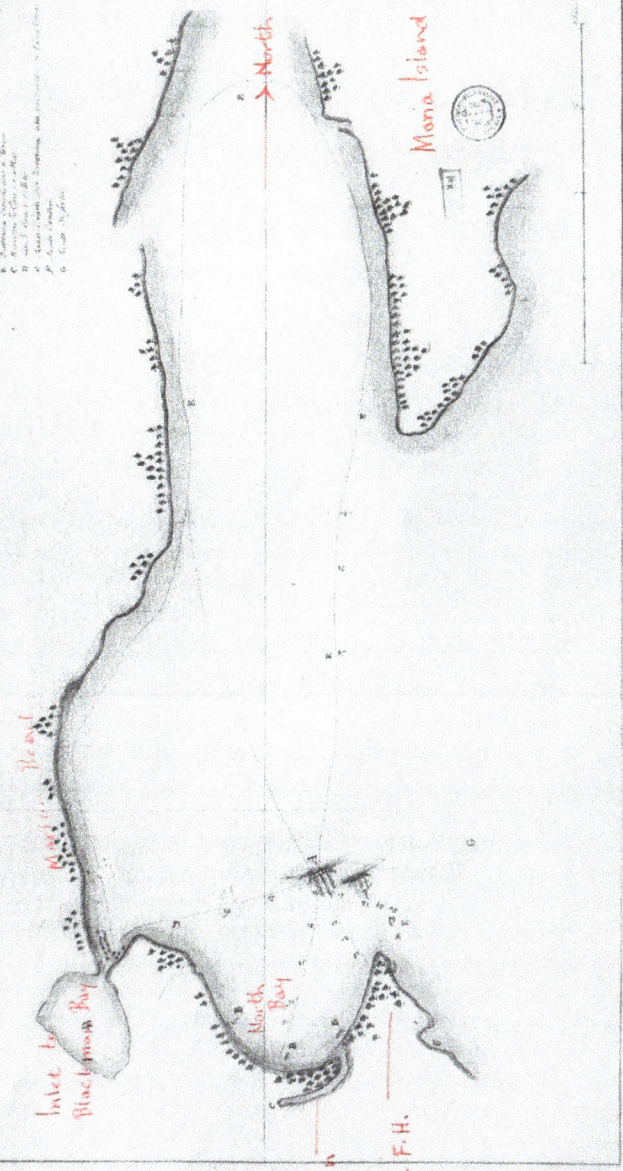

Plan de la Baye Frederic Henri, Du Clesmeur map, 1772

Du Clesmeur's chart of Marion Bay and the southern part of Maria Island (1772).

Toesman's Frederik Hendrics Bay   * see above

* Baye de Frederic Henri

Plan de la Baye de Frederic Henri Situeé a l'Est du Terra de Diemen par la Latitude Sud 12 ae........ 50'.et par la Longitude Orientale, Meridien de Paris, Observeé de 14f. 30'

North

Mona Island

Inlet to Blackman Bay

Marion Reef

North Bay

Swan Lagoon

Cape F.H.

Other officers on the two ships – Julian Crozet, Lieutenant Le Dez, Jean Roux and Paul de Montesson – all wrote personal journals that left no doubt that they deliberately anchored at Tasman's site, and that they considered themselves to be in Frederick Hendrik Bay.

So who was this Marion Dufresne whose name was eventually misapplied to this bay? He was an adventurer. He had been in command of the back-up ship when Bonnie Prince Charlie was rescued from Scotland and taken back to France; he was returning the kidnapped Ahu-toru to Tahiti (Dunmore, 1990) which resulted in him being in Van Diemen's Land. For we Tasmanians, he is notorious mostly because his crew shot and killed the first Aborigine to die in the defence of his homeland against invasion (Rochon, 1891). That was at the North Bay on 7 March 1772.

Julian Crozet's version of the Dufresne episode in 1772 is the one commonly quoted and accepted. In this version, conflict began when Marion lit a small pile of wood, apparently at the request of the Aboriginal people. Less known are the private journals of other officers of the Expedition, such as Du Clesmeur and Le Dez. A reconstruction of the events, as recorded in those journals (Duyker, 1992) leads to a different conclusion, as follows.

Dufresne carefully planned a deceptive approach to the Aborigines. The first boat carried Dufresne – he couldn't have been in the second boat because that did not arrive until after Dufresne had lit a fire. The first boat stopped some distance from the shore (beyond the surf), and two sailors waded ashore naked (presumably to show that they were unarmed and were ordinary human beings).

When Dufresne had landed and satisfied himself that he could control the situation, he gave a pre-arranged signal to the (hidden) second and third boats. What was that signal? The normal method of signalling at sea was by means of flags; whereas land signalling was usually by sending up smoke. Given that the other two boats were at each end of Two-mile Beach, was it to light a fire?

The appearance of the second and third boatloads of people, and the possibility of others yet to come (Crozet wrote of "the yawls and the longboats", indicating a minimum of four) caused panic among the Aborigines – nothing to do with the fire-lighting.

The Aborigines gave a clear indication that the Frenchmen were no longer welcome. Instead of accepting that message, Dufresne tried to outwit them by ordering his boats to be rowed quickly further along the beach – but, of course, they were outrun by the Aborigines, who pelted them with stones and threw spears. An African servant in one of the boats was hit by a spear, and the French retaliated with gunfire (one officer wrote that they were forced to fire), resulting in at least one death, the first Aborigine to die in the defence of his homeland against invasion.

What happened to the man's body? The record tells us that he was measured and washed – leading to the great 'scientific discovery' that his skin was not black but a copper colour. Did they bury him? Or leave him for his family to reclaim?

TOBIAS FURNEAUX
MUDDLES THE MAPS

~

James Cook, on his first Pacific voyage in 1770, had approached from the east, around the tip of Cape Horn. He had intended a landfall on the east coast of Tasmania – to pick up where Tasman had left off – but southerly winds forced him north to Point Hicks. He noted, though, the signs of an opening to the west.

On his second voyage, in 1773, he came across the Indian Ocean in company with the "Adventure" captained by Tobias Furneaux. They became separated shortly after the Cape of Good Hope, and the rendezvous for such a separation was a pre-arranged meeting place in New Zealand/Aotearoa.

However, Furneaux remembered that Cook had wanted to investigate Tasman's anchorage in Frederick Hendrik Bay, the so-called Van der Lyn islands and to see if there might be a strait north of Van Diemens Land. So, he decided to spend a few days in those areas, and to do that work, hoping to then meet up with Cook.

In the end, he reported to Cook, in New Zealand/Aotearoa, that he had anchored just south of Frederick Hendrik Bay, and called the location Adventure Bay; that there were four islands in the Van der Lyn group (actually Freycinet Peninsula); and that there was no strait north of Van Diemen's Land.

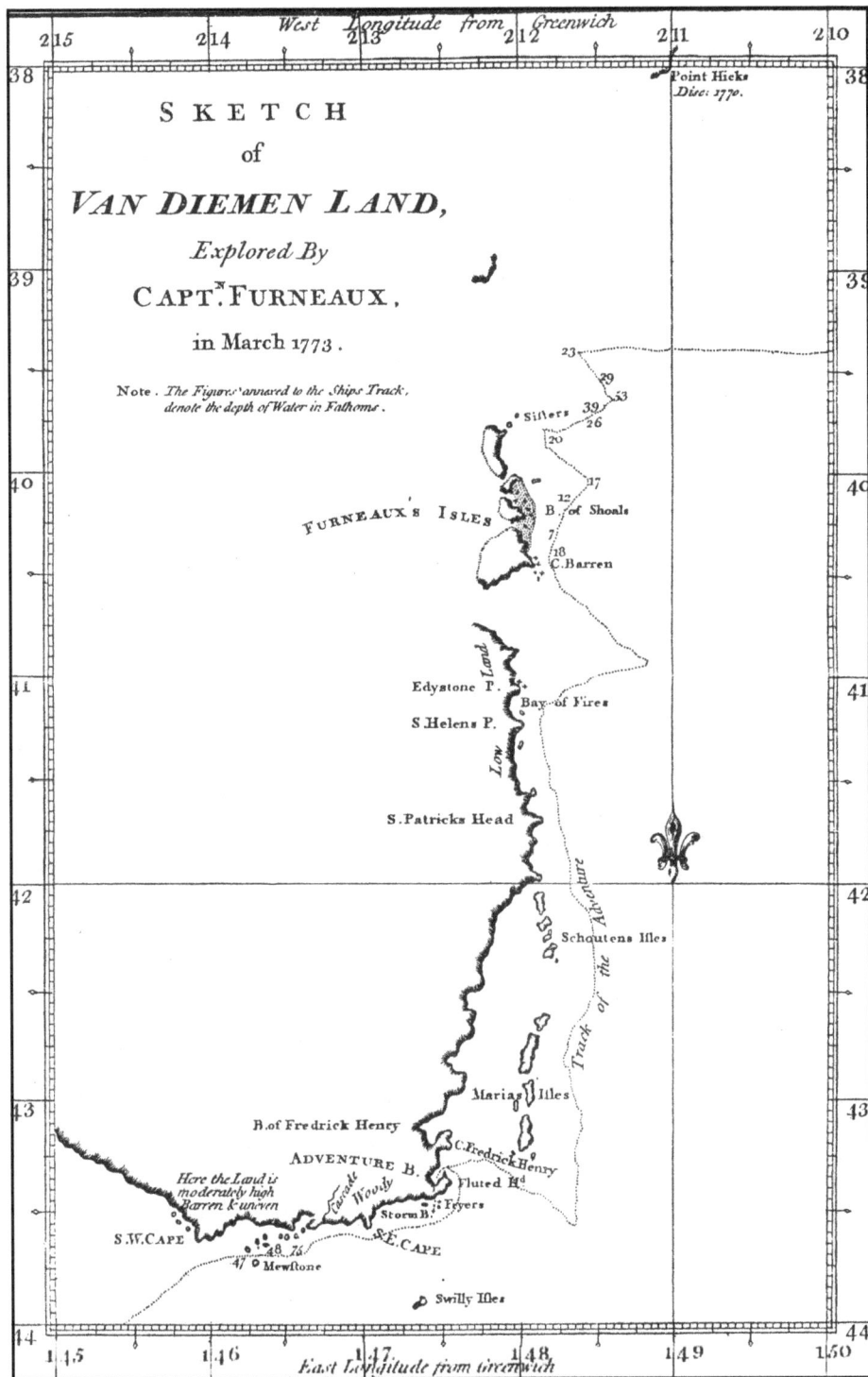

Sketch of Van Diemen Land, 1777

What Furneaux had done was to glimpse the opening to D'Entrecasteaux Channel and thought that was Storm Bay. He thought he had rounded Cape Pillar and was on the east coast just south of Cape Frederick Hendrik, whereas he had turned left one stop early and was at Bruny Island, where he named Adventure Bay for his ship.

The cape to his north he assumed to be Cape Frederick Hendrik, with Frederick Hendrik Bay on the other side of it – so put both names on his chart. Off to the north-east, Furneaux could see where Maria Island should be, but there seemed to be a few extras, so he changed the name to Maria Isles. He bestowed names and made maps, that muddled the mapping from Bruny Island to Maria Island.

He then sailed north along the east coast and took a quick look around the corner at the top end. Furneaux then got lost again in New Zealand waters, and had half his crew down with scurvy because he had ignored Cook's instructions about lime juice. At that point, Furneaux wanted to go home, and I suspect Cook was glad to be rid of him. Furneaux wrote a book about his journey, including his muddled chart.

This series of mapping blunders could have been of no consequence except that unfortunately, Cook incorporated the chart and information into his account of his voyage, thereby lending it the authority of his good name. He omitted the chart in his second edition.

Thirty years later, Dutch maritime influence had waned, and the first settlers preferred to rely on the word of the great Captain Cook rather than that of 'foreigners' like the Dutchman Tasman. Hence, Tasman's most important name, Frederick Henrik Bay, was lost to its true location and misplaced to where we see it today.

Admiral D'Entrecasteaux undertook an expedition that brought him to the Channel areas of Van Diemen's Land in 1791-92 and again in 1793. He was reputedly searching for the lost expedition of La Perouse, but he also had a team of expert mapmakers with him.

The name Cape Frederick Hendrik was shown on the chart they prepared. This name was not mentioned in Tasman's journal nor shown on Tasman's chart. However, it was on a 1726 chart prepared by Valentyn and carried by D'Entrecasteaux and Baudin. Perhaps Valentyn had access to other material since lost, or maybe he made a logical assumption that the cape cradling the southern end of Frederick Hendrik Bay would be called Cape Frederick Hendrik. So D'Entrecasteaux did us good service in at least keeping that name alive in its proper place.

Nevertheless, on leaving Van Diemen's Land in 1793, and without visiting or seeing it, D'Entrecasteaux bestowed the name "Marion Bay" in place of Frederik Henrik Bay – perhaps in order to simply honor Marion Dufresne but just as likely because it was politically important to get French names on the map.

His action violated the rules of naming rights because D'Entrecasteaux knew that Marion was not the first to see, sail over or map the bay; that was acknowledged in the chart titles "Baye de Frederic Henri". Marion would have turned in his grave – except that he didn't have one, having been killed and eaten by Maoris some three months after leaving Van Diemen's Land.

In 1802, Baudin criticised the name Marion Bay on two grounds: the water named Marion Bay is not, in fact, a bay, but an 'open roadstead'; and that Marion saw and sailed over nothing that Tasman had not already seen in 1642 – and therefore was not entitled to 'naming rights'. It was Baudin who had the delicate job of telling D'Entrecasteaux of his error.

As Marion is associated with the first killing of a Tasmanian Aborigine this makes the name unsuitable, and the location is ideal for consideration by the Aboriginal community for an offical palawa-kani name.

MATTHEW FLINDERS'
LOST CHANCE

———— ≈ ————

Flinders was born in 1774. His grandfather and father were surgeons, and it was expected of him that he would follow in their footsteps. However, Flinders wanted to be an explorer, and studied all the right subjects (including the sciences) with that aim. At 16 he joined the Navy and, after a year, was drafted into a science-based expedition transplanting breadfruit from Tahiti to the West Indies, as a midshipman under Captain William Bligh (who had studied navigation under Cook). By the end of the voyage, Flinders was in charge of all the navigation, chart records and position-fixing.

In 1794 Flinders has his first and only experience of naval warfare, when he distinguished himself at the Battle of the Glorious First of June.

He volunteered to join the ship taking the colony's second Governor (John Hunter) to Sydney. During the six-month voyage, he befriended the ship's surgeon, Dr George Bass, also interested in exploration. They reached Sydney in 1795, and Flinders (now 21) and Bass made many exploratory expeditions in the "Tom Thumb".

As well as the private voyages, Flinders was sent on some official duties doing survey work while on the colonial schooner "Francis" –

including to the Furneaux Islands, north-east Tasmania. As a result, Flinders agreed with Bass that a straight must exist, and they set out to prove it. The circumnavigation of Tasmania took place from November 1798 to January 1799.

In his monumental 1798-99 survey of the whole coastline of Van Dieman's Land, Matthew Flinders had the opportunity to re-instate historically correct names – and he did so. He struck out Furneaux's "F.H. Bay" at Seven Mile Beach and re-instated the "North Bay" of D'Entrecasteaux; and he deleted "Marion Bay" and restored Tasman's "F.H. Bay".

Flinders' chart of Bass Strait and Tasmania was published in London in June 1800. Immediately on return to England in September 1800, Flinders put forward a plan for charting the blank sections of the coastline of Australia. With strong support from Banks (who was interested in the associated botanical studies), and with the knowledge that the French had commissioned Baudin for a similar journey, the plan was quickly put into effect.

Flinders was appointed as Lieutenant-in-Command of the "Investigator" with a crew of 88, including a naturalist, a natural history painter, and landscape painter, a gardener and a miner (to assess mineral potential). His younger brother Samuel (aged 18) was Second Lieutenant, the midshipman was John Franklin (aged 15) later to become a famous Arctic explorer and Governor of Tasmania – and Flinders' cat Trim (aged 4), soon to be the first cat to circumnavigate Australia.

The "Investigator" sailed from Portsmouth on 18 July 1801, and made landfall at Cape Leeuwin, WA, on 6 December. Flinders charted in the Great Australian Bight during January, was at Spencer Gulf on 20 February, met up with Baudin on 8 April and was at Port Phillip Bay early May, and then to Sydney. After a short stay, he started off again north along the east coast and then to the west. At this point, the "Investigator" was found to be unseaworthy, so he returned to Sydney (June 1803) via the south coast.

There he embarked as a passenger aboard the "H.M.S. Porpoise" to complete the north-west survey and to return to England in order to get another vessel, but on 17 August was wrecked on a reef in the Coral Sea.

So, back to Sydney, in the ship's cutter, to arrange the rescue of the rest of the ship's passengers and where Governor King loaned him the 29-ton schooner "H.M.S. Cumberland" to make the voyage. The "Cumberland" was in poor condition after the survey was completed; therefore, it was decided to call at Mauritius for repairs.

Arriving on 17 December 1803 (one day after the Baudin ships had sailed for home), Flinders was imprisoned by the local Governor, Charles Mathieu Isidore Decaen, on the grounds that his safe-passage document specified that he was commanding the vessel "Porpoise", whereas he had arrived in the "Cumberland", and was considered to be a spy due to war having broken out between France and England.

Napoleon signed a release in March 1806, which was received in Mauritius in July 1807, but Decaen refused to act, saying that the conditions had changed. Decaen finally agreed to the release in March 1810 – six and a half years after imprisonment.

By the time he got back to England, on 24 October 1810, and finished the preparation of his material, he reluctantly accepted on the matter of Frederick Henrik Bay that the incorrect names had then become so established that it was not practicable to restore the original names. Additionally, he was in poor health and it was said that, near 40 years of age, he looked to be that of 70.

The first set of his books were hurriedly bound and taken to his home on 18 July 1814 and placed in his hands – unnoticed because he had lapsed into unconsciousness and died the next day.

Chart of Terra Australis. Sheet VI, South coast / by M. Flinders, 1798-99

The original Frederick Henricx Bay of Tasman, Lex Johnson

Boomer Creek (Water Place)

(prev. labelled "Frederyck Henricx Bay" (added by Furneaux error) 1773 Now Blackman's Bay (recent))

Frederick Henricx Bay

Now North Bay (Furneaux error) 1773 (prev 2 Mile Beach)

Visscher Is.

Cape Frederick Henricx

(prev. Prince of Wales Bay) Now Tasman Bay (recent) (site of flag-placing)

Now Marion Bay (D'Entrecasteaux) 1793

Marion Eijlandt

Sketch in the Journal of the Tasmanian Coastline in the Vicinity of the Anchorage of the "Heemskirk" and "Zeehaen", December, 1642.

The original Frederick Henricx Bay of Tasman. (developed following research in 1942-6 consequent upon confirmation of Boomer Creek as the Water Place of Tasman Exped. 1642)

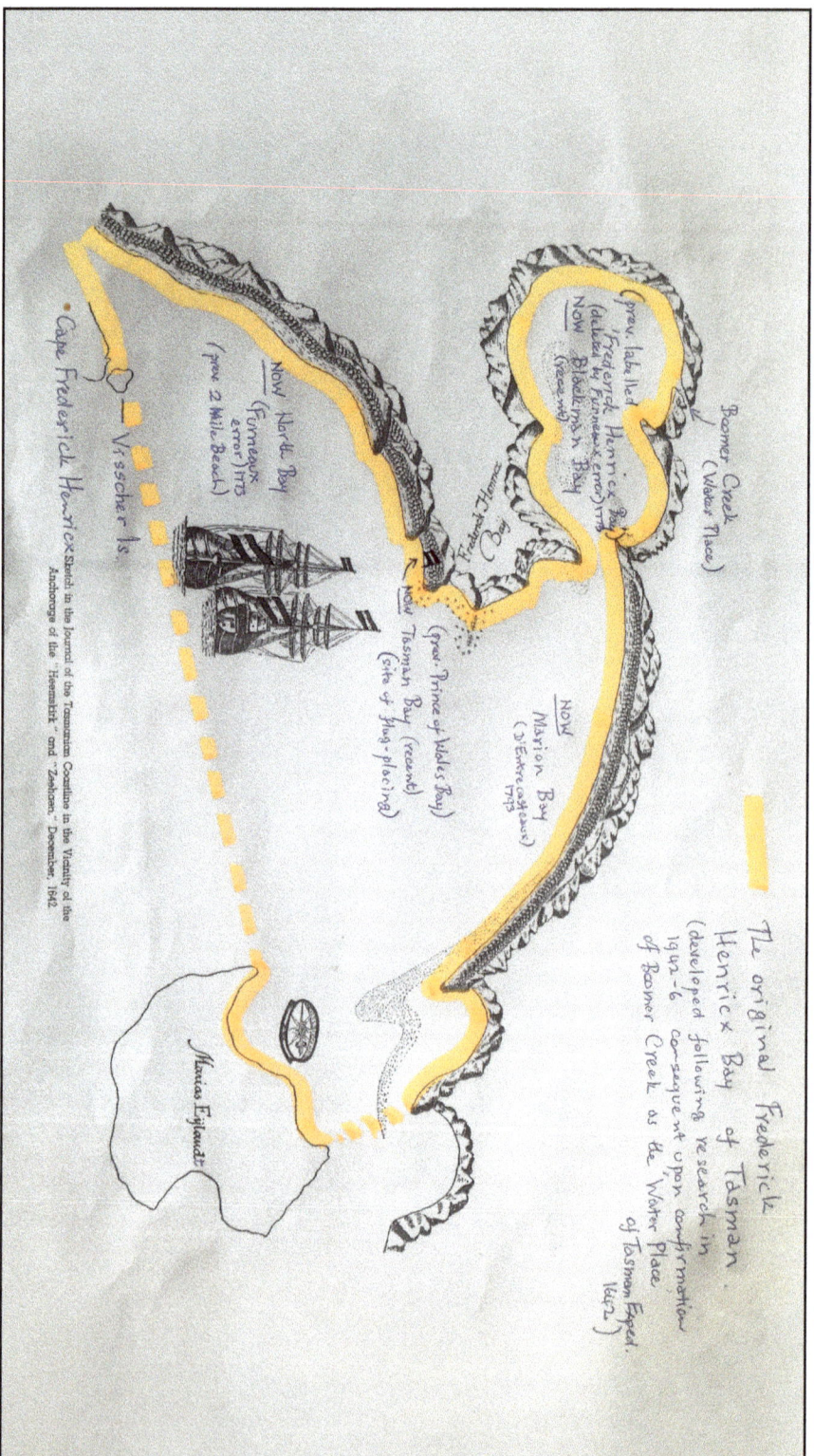

The market for the book was substantially reduced because of the French publication seven years earlier, with an English translation. The French book made false claims to land first chartered by Flinders and included mapping material that could only have come from charts Flinders had with him at Mauritius.

So, we now have Tasman's most revered name, Frederick Henrik, in a place that Tasman did not intend, and never saw; while the true site for Frederick Henrik Bay is called Marion Bay after a French pirate who was responsible for the death of the first Tasmanian Aborigine to die in the defence of his homeland against invasion.

NICOLAS BAUDIN
SUSPECTED THE TRUTH

≈

In 1799, when he was 45, Baudin put forward a proposal to complete the mapping of Australia. At that time, Britain had claimed the eastern half (and Tasmania), while the western half was still known as "New Holland" and was not settled – therefore "available".

Baudin had experience in mapping and scientific study, as displayed in previous voyages in the Indian Ocean and West Indies. He had progressed through naval ranks as an Officer of the Blue; that is, he wore a blue uniform instead of the red one worn by the regular officers (who were almost exclusively gentlemen of the aristocracy).

It probably suited Napoleon to keep the door open on occupying Australia, so the plan was approved, but he increased the scientific emphasis by upping Baudin's request for eight scientists to the 22 who actually sailed from the home port on 19 October 1800.

Fortunately, a good many of those took the first boat home after rounding the Cape of Good Hope and arriving at Mauritius on 15 March 1801.

Baudin's expedition left Mauritius on 25 April 1801 and arrived off Cape Leeuwin (in what is now WA) a month later. They mapped north along the west coast for three months before heading for

Kupang (Timor) for the winter storm season. They lost 18 men to dysentery and tropical diseases during the stay in Kupang.

Others died later during the voyage (one in what is now Tasmania) so that, in the end, only three out of the 22 scientists returned. There were similar defections and deaths among the officers, resulting in the Freycinet brothers (Henri, aged 24 and Louis, aged 22) being temporarily promoted as Lieutenant-Commanders – a rank they would not have expected to reach for another ten years.

Similarly, Citizen Peron elected himself to be the leading scientist, and constantly criticised Baudin's handling of the expedition. This antagonism between the two men was to be a major factor later as, after Baudin's death on the way home in 1803, Peron wrote the history of the voyage, using Baudin's name only once – the record of his death.

Peron himself died in 1810 (aged 35), and it was left to Louis Freycinet to complete the Atlas of maps and illustrations.

They made it to Tasmania, anchoring in D'Entrecasteaux Channel on 13 January 1802. Their records show that the next two months in Tasmanian waters helped to restore health and spirits to the weary crew and provided formidable results to scientists and navigators alike.

On 20 February 1802, when the ships were anchored off Maria Island, Captain Baudin sent off four boat parties to explore around the island; to the mainland opposite; to the north beyond Freycinet Peninsula; and to the south as far as Cape Frederick Hendrik.

His orders to Citizen Henri Freycinet, Lieutenant Commander, in charge of the southern party, included the following:

> "Upon reaching Frederick Hendrik Bay, you are to go carefully, for the sand-bars marked on Valentyn's chart do exist and are exposed at low tide. If there is not enough

water for you to examine this bay in the longboat, then you are to do it on land; but either way, you are able to explore its entire length. You must be extremely accurate in taking your bearing and must repeat them as many times as possible so that the chart of this bay and its depth may be perfect." (Cornell, 1974 p 339)

Baudin doubted the D'Entrecasteaux 'waterway' theory, and correctly reasoned that there must be a second isthmus (today's East Bay Neck) and therefore two peninsulas.

Why was it so important that the chart of Frederick Hendrik Bay be perfect? That, if necessary, Freycinet should walk around it.

To answer that we need to go back to the 1642 expedition of Tasman; the contributions of the next visitor, Marion Dufresne, in 1772; and Matthew Flinders in 1798 – and to look at the negative input of Cook's offsider, Captain Furneaux, in 1773, and Admiral D'Entrecasteux in 1792-93.

That final name gives part of the reason for Baudin's insistence on accuracy. A captain (as was Baudin), with some thought of future promotion, needed to be very sure of himself before challenging the work of an admiral in his own navy.

Peron carefully negotiated the problem by lavishly praising the D'Entrecasteaux charts, saying that they needed only a few corrections to make them perfect.

In commenting on Henri Freycinet's report, Citizen Peron made two points: "What is called Marion Bay is no more than a roadstead situated in front of Frederick Hendrik Bay (Blackman Bay)" and "Marion did not discover anything that was not already known to Tasman". However, Peron concluded:

> "…custom having always prevailed in such matters, we shall restrict the name Frederick Hendrik Bay to the little

harbour visited by M. Henri Freycinet, and give the name Marion Bay to the great Roadstead situation in front of this harbour and which extends, as have said elsewhere, from Cape Bernier in the north to Cape Frederick Hendrik in the south".

Basically, Baudin's group saw the error in the situation but were not prepared to upset Admiral D'Entrecasteaux (and the naval establishment) by correcting it.

Numerous historians and authors drew attention to the muddle, from the 1800s through to "The Australian Pilot" in 1920, and to Plomley in 1983, but no action has been taken. Perhaps the best summation was by James Backhouse Walker in one of his 1890s lectures to the Royal Society:

"By what freak of the map-makers of our Survey Department these names have been shuffled about so oddly I am quite at a loss to imagine".

Margaret and Lex at Gilsemans Bay (Photo: Shirley Johnson) *45*

Bibliography

Bach, John (ed) (1968) An Historical Journal of Events at Sydney and at Sea Angus and Robertson

Badger, Geoffrey (1988) The Explorers of the Pacific

Betts, T. (1830) An Account of the Colony of V.D.L. Calcutta

Bischoff, James (1832) Sketch of the History of Van Diemen's Land London

Bonnemains, Jacqueline (2001) Muséum d'Histoire Naturelle du Havre, personal communication

Brettingham-Moore, J. () Maritime Tasmania – A Cruising Guide with Historical Notes and Coastal Photography

Calder, James Erskine (1849) An account of those parts of Forestier Peninsula visited by Tasman Hobart Town Courier

Cobley, John (1962) Sydney Cove 1788

Colwell, Max (1970) The Voyages of Matthew Flinders Paul Hamlyn, sydney

Cornell, Christine (translator) (1974) The Journal of Nicolas Baudin Adelaide

46

Curtis, W. M. and Somerville, J. (1947) Boomer Marsh – A Preliminary Botanical and Historical Survey. Papers and Proceedings of the Royal Society of Tasmania

Dunbabin, Thomas (1922) The Making of Australasia London

John Dunmore (1990) 'Marion du Fresne, Marc Joseph' Dictionary of New Zealand Biography first published in 1990. Te Ara – the Encyclopedia of New Zealand, https://teara.govt.nz/en/biographies/1m13/marion-du-fresne-marc-joseph (accessed 25 December 2019)

Duyker, Edward (ed) (1992) The Discovery of Tasmania: Journal Extracts from the Expeditions of Abel Janszoon Tasman and Marc-Joseph Marion Dufresne, 1642 and 1772, St David's Park Publishing

Duyker, Edward (1994) An Officer of the Blue: Marc-Joseph Marion Dufresne, South Sea Explorer, 1724-1772. Melbourne, Miegunyah Press

Duyker, Edward (2005) "A French Garden in Tasmania: The Legacy of Felix Delahaye (1767-1829) in Explorations number 37 December 2004

Duyker, Edward (2005a) 'Marion Dufresne, Marc-Joseph (1724–1772)' Australian Dictionary of Biography, National Centre of Biography Australian National University, http://adb.anu.edu.au/biography/marion-dufresne-marc-joseph-13076/text23653, published first in hardcopy 2005, accessed online 26 December 2019

Duyker, Maryse (translator) (1992) "Account of a voyage in the South Seas and the Pacific beginning in 1771 … Ambroise Bernard Marie Le Jar du Clesmeur" in The Discovery of Tasmania – journal extracts from the expeditions of Abel Janzoon Tasman and Marc-Jospeh Dufresen 1642 and 1772 St David's Park Publishing

Fidlon, Paul G. and Ryan, R.J. (1980) The Journal of Philip Gidley King: Lieutenant, R.N. 1787-1790

Finkel, George (1975) The Dutchman Bold – Abel Tasman Angus and Robertson

Fitzgerald, Lawrence (1984) Java La Grande: The Portuguese discovery of Australia

Flannery, Tim (ed) (2000) Terra Australis: Matthew Flinders' Great Adventures in the Circumnavigation of Australia Text Publishing

Flannery, Tim (ed) (2009) Watkin Tench's 1788 Comprising a Narrative of the Expedition to Botany Bay and A Complete Account of the Settlement at Port Jackson

Furneaux, Tobias (1779) "Captain Furneaux's Narrative, with some Account of Van Diemen's Land" in Cook, James A voyage towards the South Pole, and round the world: performed in His Majesty's ships the Resolution and Adventure, in the years 1772, 1773, 1774, and 1775 London http://gutenberg.net.au/ebooks13/1306441h.html viewed 25 December, 2019

Gell, J. P. (1845) On the First Discovery of Tasmania Tasmanian Journal of Natural Science

Giblin, R. W. (1928) The Early History of Tasmania 1642-1804

Gilbert, W., Holland, J., & Napier, W. (1973) Eastern Island, Southern Seas Aldus Books

Halligan, G. H. (1925) Tasman's Landing Place

Heath, Byron (2005) Discovering the Great South Land Dural, NSW, Rosenberg

Heeres, J. E. (1898) Tasman's Journal of his Discovery of Van Diemen's Land and New Zealand in 1642, with documents relating to his exploration of Australia in 1644

Hemphill, Ian (2002) Spice Travels

Horner, Frank (1987) The French Reconnaissance, Baudin in Australia 1801-1803

Hughes, Wade (1987) Exploring Australia by Sea

Keneally, Thomas (2009) Australians – Origins to Eureka Allen and Unwin

Kenihan, G. H. (ed) (1964) The Journal of Abel Tasman, 1643, with documents relating to his exploration of Australia in 1644 Australian Heritage Press

King, Jonathan (2009) Great Moments in Australian History

Kuilboer, Michelle and Riviere, Marc Serge (1994) The French Presence in Australia: Sailors, Settlers and Ships

Lee, Ida (1911) A Forgotten Navigator: Captain (Afterwards Sir) John Hayes, and His Voyage of 1793" The Geographical Journal, Vol 38, No. 6 (Dec 1911)

Lord, Clive (1926) The Planting of the Dutch Flag in Tasmania in 1642

Maulte, Alfred (1889) Royal Socicty Papers and Proceedings Vol 12

Meston, A. L. (1952) Some New Aspects of Tasman's Visit to the East Coast of Tasmania in 1642 Royal Society

Moore-Robinson, J (1923) Tasman's Landing Place Mercury Newspaper 22 Jan 1923 p5

Mulvaney, John and Tyndale-Biscoe, Hugh (2007) Rediscovering Recherche Bay

National Library of Australia (2007) Australia in Maps

Pearson, Joseph (1943) Papers and Proceedings of the Royal Society of Tasmania for the Year 1942 TMAG Hobart

Pearson, Michael (2005) Great Southern Land

Perry, T. M. (1982) The Discovery of Australia: the Charts and Maps of the Discoverers and Explorers

Peron, Francois (1809) A Voyage of Discovery to the Southern Hemisphere London

Plomley, JB (1966) Friendly Mission

Potts, BM, Kantvilas, G and Jarman SJ (eds) (2006) Janet Somerville's Botanical History of Tasmania. University of Tasmania and Tasmanian Museum and Art Gallery, Hobart, Tasmania

Rienits, Rex & Thea (1968) The Voyages of Captain Cook Paul Hamlyn, Sydney

Reyenders, Peter (translator) and Gerritsen, Rupert (ed) (2009) A Translation of the Charter of the Dutch East India Company (Verenigde Oostindische Compagnie or VOC) Australasian Hydrographic Society

Reynolds, John (1964) Some Recollections of the Tasman Memorial Controversy, 1922-24 Tas Historical Research Association

Robson, Lloyd (1983) A History of Tasmania Melbourne: Oxford University Press

Rochon, Abbe A. E. de (editor) (1891) Account of Crozet's Voyage to Tasmania, New Zealand the Ladrone Islands, and the Philippines in the Years 1771-1772 translation by H Ling Roth London, http://gutenberg.net.au/ebooks13/1306431h.html#ch-06

Ryan, Lyndall (1996) The Aboriginal Tasmanians 2nd Ed

Sharp, Andrew (1968) The Voyages of Abel Janszoon Tasman Oxford

Shaw, Lindsey and Wilkins, Wendy (eds) (2006) The Dutch Connections: 400 years of Australian-Dutch maritime connections 1606-2006 Australian National Maritime Museum

Sprod, M.N. (ed) (1990) The Convict Probation System Blubberhead Press

Spencer, James (ed) (1981) A Voyage to New Holland (1699-1701) William Dampier

Tasman's Journal of the Voyage 1642-1643

Tardif, Phillip John (2003) John Bowen's Hobart Tasmanian Historical Research Association

Taylor, Peter (1990) The Atlas of Australian History

Walker, James Backhouse (1894) Abel Janszoon Tasman: his life and voyages

Ward, Russell (1982) Australia Since the coming of Man

Ward, Russell (1987) Finding Australia

(1963) Abel Janzsoon Tasman, A Bibliography The Trustees of the Public Library of NSW

Appendices

FLAGS

It wasn't until the independent regions making up the area known as the Low Countries or Netherlands united under the Prince of Orange to fight for independence from Spain that there was a need for a single flag – so they adopted the flag being used by the Prince who was the only one with a private army. The colours were (from the top) orange, white and blue. That was the world's first modern flag, displaying simple stripes instead of heraldic devices. During the late 17th century, the regions (now united as the Dutch Republic) changed the first stripe to red.

Of course, the semi-autonomous areas each had their own flag, as do the states making up the Commonwealth of Australia. One of the largest and most important areas was Holland, and its name came to be used by international traders – but it was never the official name of the nation.

TASMANIA'S NATIONALITY

According to European international law, custom and practice operative at the time, Tasman's claim over the land in the name of his head of state was valid. Therefore, on 3 December 1642, Tasmania became Dutch territory.

Sometime about the mid-1700s, Britain, as the dominant naval power, imposed upon the other nations an amendment that required claimants to enter into possession – as indicated by having their people occupy the land, fly their flag, and till the soil.

So, the Dutch claim was no longer operative when over-ridden by King George III's proclamation read at Sydney Cove on 7 February 1788, claiming all the land between the northern tip of Cape York to the southern tip of South East Cape, and westward to the 135th degree of longitude (about through Alice Springs). In any case, Britain and the Netherlands were on good terms at the time, and sharing kings, etc. so the Dutch did not demur.

Captain Cook's claim in 1770 did not operate in regard to Tasmania. Cook was an explorer of the 'old school' who claimed only the land he had seen or sailed past. So, his claim was from Point Hicks (Victoria/New South Wales border), his landfall ex New Zealand/Aotearoa, north to the tip of Cape York and inland to the Great Dividing Range.

Editor's note: This claim was based on the false legal assertion of Terra Nullius.

THE JOURNAL

First of all, let's look at the source of reliable research material about the journey. Practically everything we know about events on the 1642 Expeditions comes from the ship's Journal.

The original Journal has not been found. What we have are two handwritten copies of it, presumably made in Batavia (now Jakarta) on completion of the voyage.

One copy is signed by Tasman and has numerous illustrations and maps. It has been in the Netherlands State Archives since 1867. The other is unsigned, with only a few maps, and is in the Mitchell

Library, NSW. It is said to be a more accurate copy of the text of the original Journal. The Journal was written up daily by someone other than Tasman – probably Abraham Coomens who was Secretary to the ship's Council.

THE TREATY OF TORDESILLAS (1494)

In the 1400s-1500s, Portugal and Spain were the rulers of the seas. They had developed the art and science of building ships suitable for ocean voyages and maintained fleets of fighting ships to protect their trading routes.

The wholesale trade in spices (cinnamon, nutmeg, pepper, mace, cloves) was a good money-earner. In those times, rich people could afford the exotic flavours imparted by rare spices – and for poor people the ordinary spices disguised the taste of less-than-fresh meat and stews.

The Spanish and Portuguese explorers were treading on each other's toes in South America, and the Pope in his role as patron of the Holy Roman Empire, of which both countries were members, considered their bickering to be unseemly.

In 1494, he drew a line on a map, along the 45th degree of West longitude, and declared the Treaty of Tordesillas under which all lands to be discovered to the east of that line would belong to Portugal, and all to the west would belong to Spain – and that is why Brazilians speak Portuguese, and most of the other countries, Spanish.

At the time, no one gave much thought to the fact that the line did not stop at the poles, but continued on the other side of the globe, at longitude 135 degrees East – which happened to run through parts of the East Indies.

So, the Spaniards hastened to mark the boundaries of their territory by occupying The Philippines; while the Portuguese established themselves at Timor. The boundaries were varied a little by the amending Treaty of Saragossa (1529). In the end, both parties abandoned the Pope's idea and settled the matter between themselves, with Portugal receiving a payment of 6 million gold ducats – because The Philippines was on their side of the line – and they sold it to Spain.

That gave Portugal easy access to the traditional Arab route to the Spice Islands in the Moluccas of the East Indies, where it established a base at Timor. Spain had access to most of the Americas.

THE START OF DUTCH TRADING IN THE 1500s

In the early 1500s, the Portuguese were the first to develop extensive trading routes to the east, with a string of fortified ports including in South Africa, Goa (in India) and Macau.

Spain came into the picture some time later, with the development of the Americas, and the shipping of gold and silver from the Pacific coast via the Strait of Magellan. Magellan was actually Portuguese but was employed by Spain for the famous voyage around the south of the Americas and across the Pacific to The Philippines in 1519-21. He was among those killed by natives, but the survivors made their way back to Spain via South Africa – the first circumnavigation of the globe.

Back home in Europe, some of the Low Countries (including some of the present-day Netherlands) had become part of the Spanish Empire. In 1568 they revolted against the Spanish oppression, thus beginning the 80 Years War (1568-1648). Eleven years later, the northern provinces formed the Republic of the United Netherlands, and two years later renounced allegiance to Philip II of Spain (who had also become King of Portugal).

Philip's war with the Dutch was basically about his imposition of Catholicism on a people who had embraced the freedom to follow a religion of their own choice.

King Philip II of Spain annexed Portugal in 1581. Because of Spain's war with its revolutionary Dutch subjects, Philip closed the ports of Portugal to Dutch shipping. The Dutch had been doing very good business in picking up boatloads of spices from Lisbon and retailing them around Europe. Now Philip cut off their access to Lisbon, excluding them from the spice trade.

England had sided with the Protestant Dutch in their war against Spain and was due to be punished by the dispatch of the Spanish Armada (1588) consisting of 129 ships. The Armada had been intended to ferry a Spanish army of 20,000 soldiers in the Low Countries across the Channel to England. Sir Francis Drake was a key player in the English defeat of the Armada. Several years later, the Dutch Admiral Heemskerk was responsible for the destruction of the remainder of the Spanish fleet near Gibraltar.

The war used up the vast income from Spain's operations in the Americas to the point of bankruptcy. Spain never recovered its supremacy as a maritime nation and took Portugal down with it. As Spain and Portugal ceased to be world powers, the Dutch took control of the spice trade in the East Indies.

The Dutch undertook a massive program of building ocean-going ships and, in 1619, established a base in the East Indies with a fort at Batavia (now Jakarta) on the Indonesian island of Java – only about 600km (as the shearwater flies) from Australia's Christmas Island.

The Dutch retaliated against King Philip with a commercial and colonial war on Spanish and Portuguese interests in Asia, Africa and Brazil, until the Treaty of Munster in 1648 ended the 80 Years War. In simplified terms, the Dutch won in Asia, the Portuguese in Brazil, and west Africa was a draw. While all that was going on the Dutch had established a toehold in the Spice Islands of the East Indies.

Spices were an ideal crop for enterprising businessmen. They grew naturally on trees and shrubs tended by low-cost natives; they were easily harvested, could be dried to reduce weight and for longevity; stored and transported well; and had an established European market with no competition.

Spices were used in flavouring food, and in disguising the taste of meat that was going 'off' in a world without refrigeration or even ice-boxes. The Dutch also had vast commercial enterprises in South Africa and Brazil.

THE GREAT SOUTH-LAND

Ancient Greek geographers had a theory that there must be a huge landmass in the Pacific region in order to 'balance' the northern hemisphere land masses – otherwise the Earth would wobble or fall over. This belief persisted well into the 18th century; hence the hunt to find the Great South-Land.

THE DUTCH

The Dutch organised the first international trading companies. Originally, a group of merchants would put up the money (capital) to build a ship and pay its crew. On its return in, say, two years, the cargo would be sold, and the profit divvied up between the stakeholders – and then start the whole process again. Later, ongoing companies were formed, bypassing the carve-up on return of the ships, and paying regular dividends.

The Dutch at that time were not royalists – they did not have a King or a Queen but instead were a republican federation of semi-autonomous areas. However, they found that they were left off the invitation list when the crowned heads of Europe met to make important decisions. So, they unearthed William, whose inherited family estates included the small principality of Orange in southern France – with rights to the titles of Prince of Orange and Count of Nassau.

When England had finished its little episode of operating without a King or Queen, and Oliver Cromwell had done his dash, it found that it had run out of eligible claimants to the throne – so Prince William's son was invited to take up the job, and reigned as William III until 1702, after defeating James II at the battle of the Boyne (1690). His mother was Princess Mary of England.

One of Napoleon's last acts was to arrange for his son and daughter-in-law to become King and Queen of the planned "Dutch Kingdom", but Waterloo put paid to that. Nevertheless, the Netherlands did, eventually, become a kingdom in 1814.

THE DUTCH SHIPBOARD DEMOCRACY

In the same way that the Netherlands was a democratic republic, and the V.O.C. head office in Amsterdam was governed by a bard of Directors called The Lords Seventeen, and the Asian Office at Batavia was run by Governor Van Diemen and his ten Councillors, the Tasman Expedition was managed by a Ship's Council.

The Commander (Tasman) was Chairman and all the officers – both ships – were permanent members. If matters of crew discipline were involved, the two bosuns joined the Council. For navigational matters, the two steersmen became members and the senior navigator (Vischer) had two votes.

There are frequent reference to meetings of the Council being called (by the 'Heemskersk' flying a white flag, and the 'Zeehaen' members rowing across to it). So, when we read of Tasman doing this or that, we should keep in mind that it was no dictatorial command (such as by Captain Bligh in the Royal Navy) but a democratic decision by representatives of the 110 Expedition crew members.

NAVIGATION – LATITUDE AND LONGITUDE

Determining latitude is relatively easy. At the Equator, at noon, the sun is directly overhead. As you move south (or north), the sun at noon is not directly overhead, but off to one side – until you get to the Poles when it disappears altogether. So, an instrument that measures how far the sun is offside at noon will enable you to calculate how far you are from the Equator.

Longitudes are lines that run from the North Pole to the South Pole – there are 360 of them, representing the 360 degrees in a circle. The longitude line for zero (0 degrees) is in London (at Greenwich).

If it is noon in London, but 6pm where you are, the time difference is six hours which is a quarter of a day of 24 hours; so you must be a quarter of the way (to the East) around the globe; that is, 90 degrees East longitude.

But, obviously, the key to that is knowing when it is noon in London. THAT'S EASY – set your clock to London time and carry it with you.

WHAT CLOCK? Up until the 1750s no one had invented a reliable clock that would operate at sea.

So, they operated by "dead reckoning" – so called because if you got it wrong you would probably die.

Throw a heavy log overboard with a long string attached. It remains in the position while the ship moves away from it. Let it float behind the ship for a known period of time. Measure the length of string paid out – and do a calculation of the ship's speed. Multiply the number of hours travelled since the previous measurement – equals the distance travelled. Plot that on the chart (and enter it into the book kept for the purpose – called the ship's LOG). The string had a knot tied in it every six feet (one fathom) – hence the ship's speed in knots.

Of course, there are problems with things called currents. If you are in a current going the same way as the ship, the log might keep pace with you. Conversely, a current running against the ship might cause the log to race away at great speed when, in fact, the ship may be going backwards.

The early Portuguese route to the East Indies followed the coast all the way. The Dutch instituted a 'short-cut' from South Africa due east to the west coast of Australia, and then due north to the Indies.

The trick was to know when to turn north – and the W.A. coast is littered with wreck sites. On the other hand, one enthusiastic Dutchman (Pieter Nuyts, 1627) sailed too far to the south and ended up all the way across the Great Australian Bight. If he'd kept going for another week or so he'd have passed through Bass Strait, and have been the first European to discover the east coast of Australia, 143 years before Cook!

WIND

Ships of the 1500s and 1600s performed at their greatest efficiency when running before the wind; that is, ship and wind are heading in the same direction.

Steering to either side reduced efficiency. Sailing across the wind ('tacking') required frequent sail changes, which were a heavy demand on the sailors, and the rigging.

Experienced navigators were familiar with the world's patterns of seasonal winds and could plot a course to take advantage of them. For example, when Tasman's ships left Batavia they headed for the island of Mauritius, where they intended to carry out some repairs and replenish water. But the Company had excellent repair facilities at its home base at Batavia; and full water barrels aboard, so was there another reason?

At that time of year (mid-August), north-easterly trade winds blow across the Indian Ocean, so they could count on a following wind all the way to Mauritius. On leaving there they headed south to the 40th degree – the 'roaring forties' – with a guaranteed following wind all the way to Tasmania and beyond. All these things were considered during the plotting of the course. That work was done by the Pilot-Major Visscher, the Company's navigation expert, in the 18 months he worked on the project prior to Tasman being selected to lead the expectation.

DRINKING WATER AND COOKING

The expedition carried food and water sufficient for twelve months, but was back at Batavia in ten months, so there was never a concern about those items.

The frequent Journal references about seeking water were not because there was a shortage, but because it was traditional to mark water sites on the maps for the benefit of later expeditions; and, as a special treat – to have fresh water for a few days.

The water taken aboard at Batavia, and topped up at Mauritius, would not have been of good quality; and it was put into wooden barrels that had not been sterilised, so the normal action of bacteria would have produced a 'tainted' taste within two weeks

Water was not drunk aboard ship. Instead there was a daily issue of arack, a low-alcohol beer which would 'keep' for a year. The officers may have substituted wine.

Water was used to make soups and stews (the staple diet), thickened with flour and ships biscuits. The word 'biscuit' comes from the Latin 'bis' (two) and 'coctus' (bake) = twice baked. "Biscuit" also refers to porcelain after firing but before glazing – and that is probably a good description of a dry ship's biscuit. They were also good hiding places for weevils, and there were various methods for evicting them. Alternatively, one could obtain the benefit of a little protein by dropping the whole biscuit into the stew.

There were 60 crew on the "Heemskerck". They would have been divided into four 'watches' of six hours each. Each watch of 15 sailors would appoint a 'cook', whose job it was to collect the daily ration, and take it to the galley to cook into a communal meal for that group.

Under the Company's rules for its ships, there were 'meat days' (twice weekly) – usually salted pork; and 'fish days' (barrels of salted sardines)

Whenever the ships tied up in ports, fresh fruit, vegetables and greens were taken aboard. The crew members who collected water at Boomer Creek in 1642 also took back to the ship samples of two greens they had found to be edible – Apium prostratum (sea parsley) and samphire.

The anti-scurvy benefits of citrus fruits were not identified until the 1750s. Cook was a supporter of the experiments which led to compulsory use of limes in British ships – hence British sailors became known as "limeys".

BAUDIN AND THE PENINSULAS

Nicolas Baudin's chart-making accolade is in the final words of Plomley's 1983 study *The Baudin Expedition and the Tasmanian Aborigines 1802*.

> "The work of charting was carried out intensively, with pertinacity and at a high standard of accuracy, and Baudin saw to it that it was neither slipshod nor shirked. Thus, the charting of the east coast of Tasmania had not been completed by the time Baudin entered Bass Strait in March 1802 and then sailed westwards to survey along the southern coast of the continent, but he returned to Tasmanian waters afterwards, in winter, to continue the survey there, and only gave up when bad weather and sickness among his crew forced him to sail for Port Jackson.
>
> Let us praise worthy men: among them we must remember Nicolas Baudin."

Baudin continued mapping the Tasmanian east coast until 24 March when he crossed Bass Strait and started on the westward survey of the Australian south coast, during which time he met Flinders mapping in the opposite direction at what is now called Encounter Bay (8 April 1802).

By mid-June the ship and crews were in poor condition, and it was decided to winter in Sydney, where they stayed until 17 November. The "Naturaliste" was sent home laden with the scientific collections. Baudin bought a boat (Le Casuarina) and set off to survey in the King Island and Hunter Group from 6-27 December 1802.

Meanwhile, Governor King had received information that the French might be going to attempt settlement in the islands of Bass Strait, and possibly in Tasmania. King despatched Lieutenant

Robbins in the "Cumberland" with orders to land on each island, raise the flag, fire a salute, plant some seeds, and leave a soldier in residence.

This was because Britain had announced, in the late 1700s when she was undisputed ruler of the seas, that she would no longer recognise simply "discovering and claiming" as a full title to ownership, unless it was followed up by settlement including tilling the soil.

The British 1788 proclamation of ownership west to the 135th degree of longitude was made when Tasmania was believed to be part of mainland Australia. With the discovery of Bass Strait (1798), and Britain not in occupation of the island, it had no ownership rights under its own rules. Hence the rush to "settle" the Bass Strait islands, and to speed up the proposed settlements at Risdon and the Tamar.

In private letters to his friend Governor King, Baudin made three statements that define his personal standards:

1. Contrary to Peron's opinion that a sealing industry could be established in Bass Strait, Baudin too the view (unusual for his time) that the catch was unsustainable, and that there would be no seals left in a few years.

2. On the matter of Tasmanian status, he pointed out the loophole of no British settlement and, therefore, unextinguished rights of the Dutch.

3. BUT he also said (as a private individual) that he was unaware of any French plans for settlement, adding that he believed the French had no right to dispossess the Aboriginal inhabitants and (he wrote) "nor, I think, do you".

Baudin then moved on to Kangaroo Island in South Australia, Spencer and St. Vincent Gulfs, the coast west to Albany, and retraced his previous coverage of the west and north-west coasts by the end of February 1803. He was in the Gulf of Carpentaria during May and June.

In July, Baudin became terminally ill, the crews exhausted, and it was decided to return to Mauritius, where Baudin died on 16 September. The expedition ship "Geographe" sailed for France on 16 December (ironically, the day before Flinders arrived at Mauritius and was imprisoned) and reached home on 23 March 1804.

The live animals and plants were immediately transferred to the Empress Josephine Bonaparte at Chateau Malmaison, which was looted in 1813 when the Bourbon monarchy was restored.

BLACKMAN BAY

The plains to the south of Lagoon Bay were known to be a favorite place of the Aborigines – so were called Blackman Plains.

The watercourse draining the plains was Blackman Rivulet, and the small part of Frederick Hendrik Bay to which it emptied was Blackman Bay.

When the name Frederick Hendrik Bay was taken from us, the map-makers could not abide the blank space and gradually shifted the name Blackman Bay until it applied to the whole sheet of water; and the left-over Baye du Nord of the French (where Frederick Henry Bay had been shifted to) became North Bay in its present inappropriate location, and so began the train of events that saw Tasman's most important name transferred to a place that he never saw.

That last phrase is important because, in those days, the strict maritime tradition was that, sovereigns excepted, only a person who had seen, sailed over, recorded in his log, or mapped a feature could name it or have it named after him.

TASMAN PENINSULA

The maps made by the 1642 Tasman Expedition showed only a vague outline of what is now called the Tasman Peninsula – which accords with the fact that they saw little of it and called it 'South Cape'.

Partly misled by Furneaux's transfer of the name Frederick Hendrik Bay to its incorrect location, D'Entrecasteaux assumed that it must open into his new Marion Bay. Therefore, he guessed that there must be a channel through – about where the Denison Canal is now – and made the peninsulas into "Abel Tasman's Island".

He chose "Forestier" in honour of the French Government Minister of Marine as the second name but, unfortunately, used it for the northern peninsula, where all the Tasman contacts were made; and gave the name "Tasman" to the southern peninsula which had almost no part in the Tasman saga.

DU CLESMEUR'S MAP OF FREDERICK HENRY BAY

In the process of undertaking research for this book, the key in the top right of the map was translated for the author in 2001 by Jacqueline Bonnemains from the Muséum d'Histoire Naturelle du Havre in France. It says:

A Endroit où les vaisseaux étaient ancrés (place where the boats were at anchor)

B Batteaux descendans à terre (place of disembarkment)

C Rivière d'eau de mer (sea water river (Swan Lagoon))

D Lac d'eau de mer (sea water lake (inlet to Blackman Bay))

E Route dressée des batteaux à la recherhce de l'eau douce (route followed by the boats in search for fresh water)

F Route d'entrée (entrance route)

G Route de sortie (exit route)

The original Blackman Bay, Lex Johnson

List of Illustrations

INDEX

www.ingramcontent.com/pod-product-compliance
Lightning Source LLC
Chambersburg PA
CBHW040803150426
42811CB00082B/2387/J